Praise fo

"It's inspiring to see such a young talent like Taarini capture the essence of what it means to be an entrepreneur. Innovation fuels all we do at Intel. The world needs more entrepreneurs to tackle our toughest challenges. This book gives me hope as it engages the next generation on the value of ownership and resilience,"
Barbara Whye, Chief Diversity and Inclusion Officer and Vice President of Human Resources, <u>Intel Corporation</u>

"Driving innovation and sharing this depth of insight is quite impressive for a 13-year-old entrepreneur and author. Both youth and adults who want to launch a new venture will benefit from Taarini's systematic approach of cultivating and then measuring entrepreneurship. At the University of California San Diego, where innovation is in our DNA, we are always excited to see change-makers like Taarini push the frontiers of knowledge and share information to help others."
Pradeep Khosla, Chancellor of the <u>University of California, San Diego</u>

"This book should be required reading for every middle and high school student. An entrepreneurial mindset is the key to our future and Taarini's book is both deep and practical in how to cultivate an entrepreneurial view of the world. From covering the social and psychological barriers and how to overcome them to practical tips on pitching and fundraising, this book has it all. Coming peer to peer, from a young aspiring entrepreneur to other young

people, there is no better message and no better messenger to convey these important ideas!"
Chuck Eesley, Associate Professor and W.M. Keck Foundation Faculty Scholar, Department of Management Science and Engineering, <u>Stanford University</u>

"In a world filled with books about "how to" everything, Taarini has captured a magnetic and compelling way to communicate the entrepreneur's spirit to a cohort we old folks call Gen Z. She embraces both born and taught, and hence answers the age old question about whether innovation, entrepreneurship and leadership are innate or learned. She clearly conveys in The Young Aspiring Entrepreneur, to an age group who is still forming its way to think and act, how to invent and lead future innovation."
Ray Lane, Former President & COO of <u>Oracle Corporation</u>, Former Chair of <u>Hewlett Packard</u> and <u>Carnegie Mellon University</u>, Managing Partner of <u>Great Point Ventures</u>

"Love this book! After twenty-five years of running my own business and helping other entrepreneurs run theirs, I was amazed at the accuracy of Taarini's perception of the early struggles. At only 13, she identifies the roadblocks of social rejection, questioning your intelligence, energy drainers, and feeling you don't fit in. Her suggestions on promotion, pitching to investors, and asking big while remaining humble will enlighten even the most seasoned entrepreneur. Buy this book for young entrepreneurs, those who lead them, and yourself."

Linda Byars Swindling, JD, CSP, TEDxSMU Speaker and Author of Ask Outrageously: The Secret to Getting What You Really Want and Stop Complainers and Energy Drainers: How to Negotiate Work Drama to Get More Done

"It is amazingly precocious of Taarini to write this insightful book on entrepreneurship - it's struggles and it's rewards. Very impressed. This book should be a required reading for all aspiring young entrepreneurs. Hats off to Taarini. I will not hesitate to recommend this book to the TiE chapters globally to complement their efforts in mentoring young entrepreneurs globally."

Venk Shukla, ex-Chairman of The Indus Entrepreneurs (TiE) Global and General Partner of Monta Vista Ventures

Foreword

Taarini has wisdom and insight to share that belies her age. Her story about overcoming adversity and preserving in the face of societal expectations is inspirational. The entrepreneurial spirit is infectious and Taarini's ideas and insights can help guide not only her peers but entrepreneurs in all situations.

As a former investment banker and now as the head of Intel Capital, I have worked with many entrepreneurs and startups. The positive qualities and frameworks that Taarini outlines in this book reflect the mindset of the successful entrepreneurs with whom I have worked.

I have no doubt that Taarini will "Make Something Big."

Wendell Brooks

President of Intel Capital

Senior Vice President, Intel Corporation

THE YOUNG ASPIRING ENTREPRENEUR

by Taarini Kaur Dang

"A 13-year Old Girl from Silicon Valley shares how to Overcome Age and Gender Barriers, and Change the World through Entrepreneurship"

ASIN B07D6F8WKM

ISBN 9781982942359

Copyright Taarini Kaur Dang 2019

All rights reserved. No part of this publication may be reproduced, distributed, or transmitted in any form or by any means, including photocopying, recording, or other electronic or mechanical methods, without the prior written permission of the author, except in the case of brief quotations embodied in critical reviews and certain other non-commercial uses permitted by copyright law. For permission requests, contact Taarini Kaur Dang on LinkedIn.

About The Author

Taarini Kaur Dang is a 13-year old (eighth-grade) student in Silicon Valley. She is a Venture Fellow at SoGal Ventures which is world's first female millennial-led cross-border Venture Capital firm investing in diverse startups. Taarini is among the youngest persons to win the Young American-Indian Award which she received from the Indian Ambassador to the US Navtej Sarna for her work in Entrepreneurship. She is an invited speaker at top conferences, like Google Launchpad Female Founders Summit, Collision Conference, TiECon, ATEA, etc.

Taarini has created a Venture Capital firm called Dang Capital that will invest in companies started by Youth (below age 22) and Women (any age). She is also the Founder and CEO of Million Champs which is an organization teaching Entrepreneurship globally. Her vision is to create a community of one million young entrepreneurs to change the world. She has done an internship in 6th grade at a Silicon Valley startup called RageOn. She is a Producer's Assistant on a Virtual Reality movie Speed Kills starring John Travolta.

Taarini is the co-Founder of a female empowerment Instagram account called @ClassyWomenn which has ramped to 59k followers in 1 year across 10 countries (Iran, Iraq, India, Afghanistan, Bangladesh, etc). She privately answers questions from women around the world on their problems in life, eg how to fight domestic violence, how to tell parents to let girls continue their education instead of getting married, choose a STEM career, etc.

Taarini is also passionate about Robotics. She and her team won the California State-level VEX IQ Robotics Championship. They represented California in the VEX Robotics World Championship as 7th graders in April 2017 in Louisville, Kentucky.

Taarini has been the President of Fremont chapter of an organization called Shoe Cyclist which collects used shoes and gives them to the homeless people locally. Lastly, she just launched her online business on Instagram called ZShopClass to sell fashion dresses.

Dedication

This book is dedicated to all the young minds out there who want to change the world!

Acknowledgement

Encouragement for writing this book came from people who have helped me tremendously in my entrepreneurial journey so far, namely Intel Corporation CEO Brian Krzanich who donated his own shoes for my organization Shoe Cyclist. Sincere thanks to several people for their extremely valuable advice: Cisco ex-CEO John Chambers, Draper Associates Founder Tim Draper, Google Launchpad's Shiri Sivan and Brett Kamita, SoGal Ventures Founders Elizabeth Galbut and Pocket Sun, and the entire team at Collision Conference.

The completion of this book would not have been possible without the selfless support of several people: Wendell Brooks (Intel Capital President), Barbara Whye (Intel Corporation Chief Diversity and Inclusion Officer), Josh Walden (Intel Senior Vice President), Chuck Eesley (Stanford University Associate Professor), Pradeep Khosla (University of California San Diego Chancellor), Ray Lane (Former President and COO of Oracle), Katherine Resteiner (Chief of Staff to Intel Capital President) and Linda Byars Swindling (Author of "*Ask Outrageously*"). Huge thanks to my family and, above all, the Great Almighty for His infinite blessings!

Thank you!

Table of Contents

Introduction 19
Chapter One 22
Free yourself from social barriers 22
    Age-based stereotypes 31
    Dealing with self-doubt 43
    Chapter summary 45
Chapter Two: Challenges 49
    How to handle negative people 63
    Chapter summary 73
Chapter Three 75
How to make something big 75
    Follow the big energy, not the big idea 77
    Publicize, publicize, publicize 84
    Chapter summary 97
Chapter Four 101
How to pitch to investors 101
    The two minutes pitch 104
        The opening part 110
        The middle part of your two minutes pitch ... 122
        The closing part 129
    Chapter summary 134
Chapter Five 139
Be humble 139
    Chapter summary 152

Chapter Six 155
Measuring entrepreneurship in units 155
    Chapter summary 174
Conclusion – I did it, you too can 175

Introduction

"Begin at the beginning,... and go on till you come to the end: then stop."

—Lewis Carroll

Many school-going children want to be entrepreneurs, some are looking for just the faintest inspiration to be entrepreneurs, and they are the ones I am writing this book for. I am 13 years (at the time of writing), and I have been an entrepreneur since I was in first grade. Thirteen may not be very old. However, I have spent those years gathering a wealth of experience in how entrepreneurs work and pursue success. This book is designed to help other kids with entrepreneurial spirits. The society does not encourage entrepreneurship, at least from my experience. Even older, more experienced entrepreneurs don't find it easy not to talk of young people. The society already has some set principles and code of conduct that it expects everybody to follow, and anyone that tends to deviate is seen as thinking differently. At least, that's my story. Many times people have viewed me as going against the norm simply because I talk about changing the world all the time. They don't understand how a kid who is still supposed to be playing Call of Duty is talking of changing the world.

The above is not just my experience alone, I know there are many of us out there who have been bullied into conformity by the society and those are the ones I want to reach out to in this book. Having been an entrepreneur since my first grade, I want to share my experiences with other young entrepreneurial kids out there so they can learn how to overcome the social barriers and be who they are meant to be. Part of what you will be learning in this book includes how to overcome the challenges associated with entrepreneurship, how to make something big, and how to pitch your business and ideas to investors, among other things. In between these topics, I will be sharing my own experiences as it regards the topic.

Join me on this ride!

Chapter One

Free yourself from social barriers

"Every man of genius sees the world at a different angle from his fellows."

—Havelock Ellis

When we look around us, we notice a swarm of kids; if we call any of them and ask them what they would like to be when they grow up. We are very sure of getting a unitary answer – they all want to be doctors, engineers, or lawyers. Others would want to be musicians, actors, and actresses. But the vast majority would want to work in corporate offices all days of their lives. It is not hard to predict these replies because it is the way the society had already programmed us to be. Even parents don't help; they often want their kids to be this and to be that. They usually want a future that is secured for their kids, and that's why nobody wants to encourage their kids to be entrepreneurs; because entrepreneurship is looked upon as living a life of uncertainty.

Even kids like us who want to break the social barrier to become entrepreneurs are never taken seriously. As a kid, we are expected to be a kid and not to be thinking about abstract stuff. We are expected to still be playing prank calls, we are expected to be watching cartoons on TV, we are expected to be playing Call of Duty, and not to be thinking of how to change the world. We are viewed as someone who hasn't even seen what the world is like, so we are not expected to change what we don't know in its entirety. And these are how the kids who want to be entrepreneurs are bullied into conformity. This is true even for older entrepreneurs. But all these are nothing but challenges that can be overcome as far as one has the right mindset. If your mindset is to change the world, to start a business, then you should never think of going back for any reason.

For example, I was in first grade when I wanted to become an entrepreneur. I wanted to change the world. I had ideas; no one took it seriously except for my parents of course.

My friends thought I was crazy; my teachers thought I was weird. I felt smart but my grades didn't show it. Maybe that's why everyone thought I was different. But I was often ignored, I was often made fun of, I was often bullied not because of my appearance per se, but because of my ideas, because of how I thought of the world, and that really bothered me. I really wanted to change the world. I knew I could, and I knew that someday I would, and someday I'll make a difference so everyone would like to learn from me.

When kids used to play on the playground I used to be all alone thinking about how I would make the world a better place; I used to be alone away from everybody and isolated. I had started reading entrepreneurship books, started talking to my parents about recent organizations and companies and what their faults were and what's good about them, etc. I used to love to visit entrepreneurship events with my dad. I used to watch TV shows like Shark Tank to understand business more. I always heard that great people were never that great when they were young. They were looked down upon in the society. I used to start thinking about that of myself. Because everyone thought I was different, everyone thought I was weird because I used to read entrepreneurship books and learn more about that.

My story above is not different from what most young persons with an entrepreneurial spirit out there feels. When you are younger, people want you to take your studies seriously, enjoy your childhood and grow up to take jobs, earn salary monthly, pay bills and die. But for many of us, life is worth way more than living to pay bills without leaving any significant impact. We can't just be bullied into conformity, and that's why I am writing this book. As I have been reiterating, I am writing to inspire young people who have ideas to not let their ideas slide because of what the society thinks of them; because even the big names you and I hear of today in the world of entrepreneurship all had a time when their ideas were castigated and made to look foolish. It is just plain human nature. Once you try to disrupt the natural flow of events and things, people kick, and if you don't have a thick skin, you will be forced to conform.

Imagine what would have happened when the first people who discovered email messaging service talked about their idea with people. They (the people around them) must have looked at them as people who were mad. They would have asked themselves, *"Why do we need to send emails when we have postal service."* They would have also said things like, *"your ideas are dead on arrival."* And they must have done all that because they were already too connected to the old ways of doing things that they didn't want to give change a chance. In the business of buying and selling, it is called buyer inertia, where buyer rather chooses to continue buying from a particular seller instead of seeking out better options. Nevertheless; in the end, even the most vocal resisters of change often move with the change. And that's why it is important that you never get swayed by people's initial rejection of your ideas and thoughts.

When they talk about your age, it is because they already have a preconceived notion of how old someone should be before making any meaningful impact in the world. If they talk about how you are not brilliant, it is still because of unnecessary stereotypes that should be discarded. In truth, the age of someone doesn't have anything to do with the ideas that the person is nursing. In this digital age, people of all ages are now exposed to the same level of information, and there is no reason why young people shouldn't exploit the opportunity to nurture their ideas. First, young people just like myself need to, first of all, make up their minds to be entrepreneurs even in the midst of opposition and resistance. It starts with a change of mindset.

Mindset is everything; if you must be successful in anything in this life, you must have the right mindset. Unfortunately, the society tries to make us have the wrong mindset so as to limit our potentials. It happened to me; at a time, the taunts were beginning to get to me. I was thinking, *"Should I just forget about this entrepreneurship thing and be like every other kid out there?"* But each time these thoughts came to my mind, I found something positive to occupy my mind with, and that's how I overcame the negative mindsets. If you are truly serious about being an entrepreneur, the first thing you need to do is to reprogram your mind to stop believing established stereotypes. Overcoming some of the stereotypes wasn't easy for me at all, you can do the same.

Age-based stereotypes

First, age stereotype is the major one that young entrepreneurs often face. As I said earlier, I suffer the age stereotype a lot myself. Many times, people just hear me and conclude that a little kid has nothing to offer. They think I shouldn't bother depriving myself of my childhood as if I ever told them I was missing anything. Because of the age stereotype where everybody believes that nothing serious would come out of a little kid, you will find it difficult earning the trust of people and getting them to buy into your idea. In my case, not even my teachers deemed it necessary to want to listen to me. Everyone just thinks I should just face my studies and get good grades instead of thinking of abstract things. Truly the age stereotype is going to affect you, and it is your responsibility to try to do your best to over it.

How to counter age-based stereotypes

1. be of good conduct

The first step I took towards countering age-based stereotype as an entrepreneurial kid was to keep maintaining good conduct and respect even those who do not have an ounce of respect for what I do. People are going to want to put you off, and they expect you to call them out so they could have something to validate their earlier claims that a kid would not have something meaningful to offer. It is always a trap and the earlier you don't fall into the trap, the better. When you are talking about your ideas and they, in their usual sense call the ideas stupid, try not to get angry, rather; try to diplomatically make them see that your ideas are not as stupid as they think.

2. Treat people like you want to be treated

A good way of guiding your behavior is to treat people the same way you would like them to treat you. Normally, you would want people to treat you nicely, so, treat them nicely too. This may not always be easy, but you are trying to counter the age-based stereotype that says that you are a kid who shouldn't have ideas.

By treating people right, you are building their confidence in you, and it won't be long before they start realizing that you may indeed have something to offer the world.

3. Stand firm in your ideas

Besides treating others in the same measure you would want them to treat you, you also want to believe in yourself and stand as firm as possible when others try to mistreat and misunderstand you because of your age. Be confident in your abilities, ideas, and thoughts and watch the way others will start recognizing those ideas and ambitions. The truth is that if you don't believe in yourself, nobody will believe you. The major reason why people tend to doubt the abilities of entrepreneurial kids is that they want you to prove yourself first before they follow. In the system of the world, kids are people known to have wavering thoughts and ideas, so people want to know that the idea you are trying to sell them isn't just one of those transient dreams that get buried as days go by. Once you have proven yourself and asserted your commitment to your dreams and ideas, people soon forget that you are a kid and begin to flow with you.

In addition to age-based stereotypes, you are also going to face social rejection. In life, people are likely to ostracize you especially if they feel threatened by the things you do. It happened several times throughout history, those who brought the significant changes we are enjoying in the world today were all victims of social rejection at one time in their life or the other. The simple reason is that people tend to hate what they don't understand, and instead of making efforts to understand that particular thing, they simply hate it. As a kid who is passionate about making an impact in the world, I face these social rejections every day. From my class teacher who thinks who is not sure what to think of me to my classmates who think there is something simply wrong with me, the list is endless. Not everybody wants to understand why I am not particularly interested in doing the things that other kids are doing. Some even think that I feel highly of myself for daring to be different, and the result I get is social rejection.

There are times when I talk about running businesses and breathing life into ideas, and people look at me and don't understand why a kid shouldn't just go to school, get good grades and work as a regular employee. Being rejected and ostracized for what you believe can be overwhelming for anyone not to talk of a kid with fragile emotions, and if you don't handle the rejection well, you may end up being bullied into conformity, making you leave your ideas, thoughts, and dreams. Now, how was I able to handle social rejection? The first step I took towards handling feelings of rejection and isolation was networking with other young people who have similar mindsets.

There are entrepreneurship clubs littered everywhere, and some of these clubs only have entrepreneurs as members. Such clubs are grand avenues to network and socialize with people of like mind. If you search carefully, you will find one of such clubs in your local environment. If you don't see one, you can create for yourself and others. After all, as an entrepreneur, you should also have excellent leadership skills. Create an entrepreneurship club where you bring budding entrepreneurs together to share ideas and to have a sense of belonging.

I have my own entrepreneurship club at Basis Independent, Silicon Valley. I have been leading the club comprised of 5 startups, and I am looking to open more chapters too. The reason is that I am particularly passionate about bringing entrepreneurship to k-12 students because I believe that young minds can change the world. Entrepreneurship clubs like the one I am leading is a great place for young entrepreneurs to come together and share ideas, and to have a sense of belonging since they are being looked upon by the society as people who are weird.

So, as a young person who is passionate about entrepreneurship and who is also looking to overcome social rejection, your best bet is to join entrepreneurship clubs and join other young and promising minds to network better. In the clubs, you are going to meet people who think as you do, and you won't feel rejected. As I mentioned earlier, if there is no such club around you, start one, identify other young entrepreneurs around you and get them to join the club.

Besides helping you overcome social rejection, the clubs will always be an avenue for you and other young entrepreneurs to share your personal experiences, ideas, and dream with people who understand you and who are supportive and will encourage your ambitions, something the dream killers out there will never do for you.

Your family will also be a source of succor when you are suffering social rejection. Even if every other person rejects you, your family can never reject you, they will always be willing to assist you, and hence, you should develop a good relationship with them. My family, for instance, have always been a great source of courage and support. They seem to be the only people who understand me. They are always there to support, and they are always ready to go over the details of my ideas with me. I talk to them about my passions and ideas, and you too should develop a good relationship with your family. They are the first to buy into your dreams, and if you have successfully gotten them to buy into your ideas, you will become less observant of what others think about you.

Once you have your family behind you and also have some great young minds with whom you share ideas, feelings of rejection will slowly subside with.

Dealing with self-doubt

Another thing I believe greatly affects young entrepreneurs negatively is self-doubt. This occasional feeling of self-doubt is not unconnected with the way the society treats young entrepreneurs. Knowing that you have the ideas that can change the world can be very satisfying, but the thought of how to bring life to these ideas can also cause you to experience anxiety, stress, and self-doubt in the process. As a young entrepreneur, it is natural to have days when you feel so down and begin to doubt yourself due to the stress and pressure you have been passing through. These times, what I normally do is to read lots of books about entrepreneurship. Nothing rekindles our minds like reading about the exploits of people who have toed the path we are currently toeing. It refreshes our minds and gives us a hope of a brighter future. I have a lot of these entrepreneurship books at my disposal, I invest money to buy them, and I make out time to read them especially when I am beginning to doubt myself due to the actions of others around me.

Besides reading books to rekindle your passion, you can also review your goals and your dreams. Remember the future you want to create for yourself, remember the myriads of problems in the world that need a solution and pull yourself out of the dungeon of self-doubt. Now, take your mind off of those things that are making you doubt your abilities and focus it on the things that help you reaffirm your faith in your dreams and aspirations. When you do, you can make sure you channel your thoughts and deeds into things are in line with your goals and aspirations.

I must admit that being an entrepreneur is very stressful and most times, it can take its toll on you, but regular exercise and medication can help you overcome this stress, so it doesn't metamorphose into some other thing like self-doubt.

Chapter summary

In this chapter, we have been looking at the various ways that social constructs tend to limit the potentials of entrepreneurial kids and I have been able to address some of the best ways I have been able to overcome these stereotypes.

As an entrepreneurial kid, no one is ever going to take you seriously until you have proven beyond every reasonable doubt that what you are nursing is way beyond the transient childhood fantasies that almost every kid have in one time of their life or the other. At most, the only people that may believe you are your family members. It is your responsibility to carry on even amidst the age-based stereotypes and the occasional feelings of self-doubt. Network with other kids that have similar passions and discuss ideas; that's an excellent way to overcome the social rejection you could be subjected to in your classroom and your peer gatherings.

Remember, people will always look at you as someone who is weird if you keep telling them that you have ideas that can change the world.

It is not strange for people to hate things they cannot understand. Since it will be difficult for them to understand how a kid who should be playing Call of Duty is going to change the world, they will definitely hate on you and call your ideas bluff. Never mind, after all, everyone who had ever achieved something significant in this world once faced similar resistances until their inventions became so irresistible. Similarly, you have to keep striving until you have achieved those dreams.

Apart from these stereotypes, there are also other hardships and challenges that young entrepreneurs face, I am going to talk about the particular ones I faced and still facing and how I have been tackling them in the next chapter.

Chapter Two: Challenges

"It was so risky and so scary, and yet at the same time, so beautiful. Maybe the truth was, it shouldn't be easy to be amazing. Then everything would be. It's the things you fight for and struggle with before earning that have the greatest worth. When something's difficult to come by, you'll do that much more to make sure it's even harder -if not impossible- to lose."

— **Sarah Dessen**

In the last chapter, I talked about how the society doesn't want you to be an entrepreneur and how the various social constructs work together to frustrate your efforts. That chapter started getting so long, so I have to continue talking about the challenges that I faced as an entrepreneurial kid and how I was able to overcome those challenges in this chapter. Through my experiences, you will learn one or two things that can help propel you ahead of haters and challenges.

As I have been saying, the journey of entrepreneurship is not an easy one; you are bound to meet obstacles on the road. From the teachers who think you are not good enough to the classmate who thinks you are feeling too high. To me, I usually see all those challenges as stepping stones to where I want to be, while other people may see them as stumbling blocks. I believe that when the road gets tougher that it is the tough who gets going. That was something I always heard as a child when I started learning and had tests.

The truth is that the society can never accept you for who you are because it already has some predefined sets of values it wants you to imbibe. It already has a specific pattern of doing things that it wants you to follow, and when you try to deviate from this pattern, you are looked upon as a rebel. As a kid, you are expected to go to school, not to question anything, take in all you are being taught, take your studies seriously, graduate with good grades; proceed to find a job, earn money, pay bills and die. But there are many of us who are never comfortable following that pattern, and that's why we are trying to challenge the status quo, because if you want a change, you have to initiate the change you desire; no one is going to hand over the change you want to you on a platter of gold.

To buttress what I just said in the last paragraph, let me share my experience of what happened when I was in 2nd grade. I had everyone around me at that time including friends, acquaintances, literally, everyone around me that used to make fun of me because of my appearance. I was not a person who is so particular about the way I look; to me, what people have in their head is better than their outward appearance any day, any time. I believe that people shouldn't concentrate more on their outward appearance, but instead, should pay more attention to the development of their inner self, their inner abilities, so that those potentials they are developing can one day make their outward appearance the most irresistible. So, I paid less attention to my appearance; people were using that to taunt me and make fun of me.

Furthermore, they also taught I was not cut out for entrepreneurship since I was bad at school. I said earlier that I used to be bad at school. People couldn't understand how someone like me who isn't very great at school can become an entrepreneur. In fact, whenever I said I had ideas that could change the world, they would laugh at me and call me buff. Many times, I felt I wasn't doing the right thing even though I knew everything I was doing was right. They were projecting really negative energy, and I had to distance myself from them before the negative energy they were projecting starts manifesting negative things in my life.

I started distancing myself a lot from everybody around me. Not only was I distancing myself from them, but I was also distancing myself from the things they do. I distanced myself away from Harry Potter and Percy Jackson books. I also distanced myself, although not much from comic books and superheroes. I found solace in exciting books about entrepreneurship such as *entrepreneurship ethos* by *Jarie Bohlander*. That book is a great book and I recommend it to anybody that wants to take their entrepreneurship journey seriously. I learned a lot from the book, and I have continued to apply all the things I learned in the book and the many other entrepreneurship books I read up till today.

In the 6th grade, there was this boy in my class who used to say women can't be entrepreneurs, he would say that women can't be CEOs. He would buttress his points by trying to point out that all the CEOs are men. That assertion used to get me so annoyed; in fact, there were many other people like this boy who didn't believe that I could become something worthwhile, a leader, or a CEO. They are already used to the system of the world where only one thing is expected of a woman, where a woman is not expected to dream big. But I was not a part of that system, I wanted to change things, I wanted to do great things, and I was training myself to get to that point of being an authority to be reckoned with. This aspect of training was one that most people didn't seem to get; they thought that for me to be a leader or a CEO; that I have to be really good at this, and great at that not minding that I was still in training.

One day I was with this particular boy that was usually at the forefront of telling me that I can't be a CEO because I am a woman, I took a magazine that had a front page of *Elizabeth Holmes*, the female CEO of the company, *Theranos*, and I shoved it into his face once. And he was shocked that I did that. (BTW, I admired Elizabeth Holmes at that time a lot but given the recent issues, I am not sure if I look up to her anymore.) As an entrepreneurial kid, and especially a female one, you are bound to meet really nasty people like the boy I just described. You should be able to identify them whenever you find them and don't always waste time to put them in their place. If you don't put them in their place, they will definitely dampen your zeal and make you lose your passion and enthusiasm. Such people project a lot of negative energy and you don't want them around you. The people you want are those that are full of positivity. Negative people will kill your zeal and make you lose faith in your ideas.

In 7th grade, I joined a robotics Club in my school only because all my friends were joining it. We had a team leader whose name I don't want to mention for obvious reasons. This leader used to boss me around; thinks she is the greatest; thinks she was the best and that no one could compare with her. She was the teacher's favorite, not just the teacher's favorite; she was everybody's favorite. Naturally, I felt intimated by the way everybody just seemed to be all over her; I felt I could never be an entrepreneur since I wasn't everyone's favorite as she was; I also felt I could never come up to her standards. With the whole attention she was getting, she was just looking down on everyone. She was looking down on me too; she thought I was weird, the same way every other person was thinking, and the fact that she was my competition even made matters worse. Like every competitor, she started spreading rumors about me; mean rumors that really hurt me from inside. The rumors made me feel bad about myself, and that made me really annoyed. From the experience, I was able to come to one conclusion, people will hate you for not conforming. I did not conform to the Club's way of doing things; naturally, I don't like following the path that every other person is following. As expected, people will hate you for daring to be different. It happens to me all the time, and overcoming this hate and not allowing it to get to you is one of the challenges that entrepreneurs, especially young entrepreneurs like myself face on a daily basis. As I have been reiterating, the whole essence of the unruly behavior towards you is simply to make you abandon your dreams, and once you do, you will be helping them be happy that their plans worked.

There was another major time in my life when I encountered some difficulties because I was going against the status quo; that was in my 7th grade. Like most teenagers, my 7th grade was the time where popular kids and everything forms in your school. At this time, everybody is at a competition to outdo the other, to be accepted. You want to change yourself, you don't feel secluded, you want to be a part of them because you want to fit in and everything. Like others, I had a popular squad who didn't care about learning about new stuff. It was a huge distraction because all they cared about was makeup dances and all these stupid teenager things. As an entrepreneur, all these are distractions from your normal life. The interests of most other kids around is definitely going to be different from your own interests. And as they run after their own interests, you should leave them and run after your own too. If you are passionate about something, you should run after it, breathe it, and live it. It is only through living your passion that it will become part and parcel of you. It is okay if you are distracted for some time like I was about how to be popular, how to be great, how to be the best. But you have to understand that it is wrong, you should do everything possible to avoid distractions.

All along, I have been sharing the experiences I have had with negative people; people who have nothing meaningful to contribute to your life but negative energy. Even though you need to avoid these people by all means, their criticisms of you and your activities can most times help you become a better person. But that can only happen if you know how to handle them properly; if you don't know how to handle negative people, they may end up pulling you down with their negativity. So, in the next couple of paragraphs, I want to talk about how I have been handling haters and negative people successfully, and how you too can handle them.

How to handle negative people

Set boundaries

The first step towards handling haters and negative people is to set a boundary around yourself. Like the boy that wanted to make sure he frustrates my entrepreneurship ambition in my 6th grade, haters are everywhere and they are going to pull you down to their level if there is no sort of boundary between and them. I mentioned earlier that I got a magazine that had a front page of *Elizabeth Holmes*, the female CEO of the company, *Theranos*, and I shoved it into his face once. That was my own way of shutting him out and setting a huge boundary between us. I didn't want his negative energy to seep into my life and affect my attitude, affect my outlook on life, and I had to do something really fast. I set limits and made sure that there was some sort of distance between me and negative people. Yes, this action of mine made them spread rumors about me the more, but did I care? No. I was more concerned about weeding out their negativities than I was about gaining their love. There were times I needed to be inexcusably around these negative people, and I made sure that those are the shortest periods of contact I have had with anyone. When I was in the robotics club in my 7th grade, I mentioned earlier that the leader of the club then was so full of negative energy and found my character weird because it didn't rhyme with her presumed notion of acceptable behavior. During my time in the club, I made sure I had just little contacts with her, and our conversations for those times were always very short. You can't control the negative behavior and attitude of other people but you can control whether or not you engage them.

Block complainers

You also need to block complainers from your life; these people will never find anything good about your actions and ideas. At all times, they are always out to point out problems and give a million reasons about how and why your ideas will fail. They don't think of solutions, neither do they offer solutions. They are only interested in making sure that they frustrate the solutions you are thinking. Don't allow them to suck you into their emotional pity party, that's the only thing they are good at. Identify these set of people in your class, in your groups and avoid them at all costs. Only deal with them if you absolutely must.

Choose your battles

Not every battle is worth fighting; imagine that you are traveling on the road and you stop to engage anybody that looks your direction. Certainly, you would never reach your destination. As an entrepreneurial kid, a lot of people are going to keep irritating you, but you can't keep engaging them all the time. If you engage everyone that irritates you; you will only come off as argumentative, and once you become argumentative, you will be welcoming negativity into your life, and that's not what you want. I have since learned to select my battles; there are times people look me in the face and tell me that I can never become a CEO, I just look them in the face and move on. There are better things I should be doing other than arguing whether I could become a CEO or not. Not every comment deserves my attention; there are times that really nasty people may engage you in a controversial topic with one thing in mind – to sap your energy. There are times they are going to say really nasty things about you. So, should you fight them? The answer is no, always try as much as possible to walk away from unnecessary conflict. There is no point in engaging someone that will never see things from your own perspective? So, it is better you just don't engage them at all. Choose your battles and you will be respected for taking the high road.

Don't over analyze the situation

How many times did people spread rumors about me? How many times did they say unfounded things about me? Uncountable times. As a kid, there were times I wanted to let the negativities get to me, those were the times I started considering being like everyone else, the times I started considering being popular. I was considering all these things because I was over analyzing the situations around me. Everyone else around me were doing teenage stuff, I was the only one that seemed to be different. I was over analyzing the situation and wanted to join the bandwagon.

The truth is that negative people and haters can often behave in the most irrational manner and you will be doing a great disservice to yourself if you try to make sense of their actions. I tried to make sense of their actions at a point in my life and the result wasn't very pleasant. Try as much as possible to prevent yourself from becoming emotionally invested in their issues.

Develop a support system

In the previous chapter, I talked about joining entrepreneurship clubs around you or creating one if there are none near where you live. Such clubs will give you the chance to build a network of positive and like-minded people. I have my own entrepreneurship club at Basis Independent, Silicon Valley. I have been leading the club comprised of 5 startups, and I am looking to open more chapters too. Entrepreneurship clubs like the one I am leading is a great place for young entrepreneurs to come together and share ideas, and to have a sense of belonging since they are being looked upon by the society as people who are weird. As a result of the influence of the negative people that surround you, you will always need help and it is left for you to know the exact times to seek help. When you find yourself being overwhelmed by emotions, that's the time you need to get to your support system. Call someone who has similar passions that you have, a mentor and calmly explain the situation. Many times, all you need is a little word of encouragement from someone that believes in you to be able to pick up your broken pieces.

Embody positivity

As an entrepreneur, you have a duty to make sure that you live and breathe your ideas. It is these your ideas and passions that should occupy your thoughts at all times, and they are the things that should always give you happiness at all times. If you let your ideas and passion be your main source of happiness, you will be radiating happiness from within and you won't even have time to notice anyone's rude or negative comments about you. Once you don't have time for people's negative comments, the comments will not bring you down or affect how you view yourself. Limit your time with negative individuals in your life by remaining positive at all times. Once negative people find out that they can never have anything on you, they will fall away naturally.

Chapter summary

In the previous chapter, I talked about how social constructs tend to limit young entrepreneurs, in this chapter, I focused more on how to handle negative people as an entrepreneur. In recap, I can say that the whole idea of this whole chapter is to block yourself from the haters. There are a lot of people that are going to come your way. There are people who are going to be out to put you down, make you feel at your worst, bully you; but you have to learn to ignore them. It is your fight at the end of the day, not theirs and you know what? 10 years from now, you will be much better than them.

To block yourself from haters and negative people, you need to set boundaries around yourself and them, choose your battles, and most importantly embody positivity. Once you have been able to deal with social constructs successfully and also succeeded in blocking off haters, you are set to make something big. The next chapter is dedicated to how to make something big.

Chapter Three
How to make something big

"First comes thought; then organization of that thought, into ideas and plans; then transformation of those plans into reality. The beginning, as you will observe, is in your imagination."

— ***Napoleon Hill***

Every entrepreneur wants to make something big. A billion-dollar question that every entrepreneur asks is, *"how do I make something big?"* Every entrepreneur asks the question and every entrepreneur seeks the answer to the question. The reason why everybody asks that question is what I call the "*spirit of Oliver Twist.*" Oliver was a child protagonist in the popular novel, *Oliver Twist* by *Charles Dickens.* In the novel, Oliver was described to have asked for more soup at one time when his soup was not enough and he was whipped for daring to ask for more soup. From that scene, the phrase was coined to mean someone who always asks for more.

In life generally, people are often caught asking for more. When entrepreneurs create something, they want more, and by more, they want to make their creation really big. When farmers cultivate, they want more harvest. Typically, one would think that the millionaires and billionaires of this world should be resting from chasing more money already. But that never seems to happen, because we are all possessed by the spirit of *"Oliver Twist."* Because we want more, all of us are always striving to get more. Billionaires are looking to make more money. Farmers are always on the lookout for the best-improved farming practices that will increase their farm yield, and entrepreneurs are always looking to create something big. Because we are talking about entrepreneurship, our main focus in this chapter will be how to make something big as an entrepreneur.

Follow the big energy, not the big idea

As an entrepreneur, for you to make something big, you have to start off with an idea that you truly believe in. then breathe through it, live through it, sleep through it, and do everything you can to execute the product. This may sound basic because literally, every entrepreneur knows that he or she needs an idea. But how many know that they need to live through the idea to make it come to life? Very few. Many times, the idea that may seem stupid and small maybe the one that would later grow into something big. Look at Netflix for instance, in 1997, Netflix founders only thought of a way of shipping DVD through email so as to make it easy for everyone to have access to DVDs. The idea must have seemed small at that time. They would have thought to themselves: *this is a crazy and small idea, we should forget about it and do something really big like just setting up a huge record store.* But no, they took up the small idea, lived through it, slept through it, and today we are all enjoying Netflix because some guys didn't discard a small idea in 1997.

What about *Mark Zuckerberg*? When he created *FaceMash* that would later metamorphose into the *Facebook* that we are all enjoying today, it was just a simple idea, but he breathed life into the idea and made it something really big that today we count a day as incomplete if we have not visited Facebook to see what friends are posting. In one of his interviews, Mark admitted that he never expected Facebook to grow so big. He simply had a small idea and created something big out of the small idea.

A mistake that I see many entrepreneurs make most of the times is wanting to create something big from the get-go. It never works that way. Even if it becomes possible for you to conceive an idea that would grow so big overnight, there are high chances that you would have hard times managing the complexities that would arise. So, first, you have to take that small idea, breathe life into it, grow it and grow with it. By growing with it, you become part of the idea, so that when it becomes really big, you won't have problems managing it.

Do not forget that making something big is never a one-shot deal. Even though the idea may be a small one, there is no guarantee anywhere that says the idea may not fail. If the idea fails, don't panic, pivot and get back on your feet. Almost all the great entrepreneurs failed at their first attempts at creating something meaningful. The information is littered everywhere on the internet, and you can read it up, I don't need to start repeating their stories. But the bottom-line is that making something big is not a one-shot deal. If you understand that *Henry Ford* failed many times before he founded the Ford Motor company that we all know today, and if you understand that our very own *Bill Gates* and

Paul Allen started a company called *Traf-O-Data* that didn't work out before creating Microsoft, you would understand that making something big is never a one-shot deal.

Many times, entrepreneurs are caught asking the question, *"is there a perfect idea?"* the answer to that question is no. For you to call something an idea in the first instance, you must have identified a pressing problem that you want to solve with the idea. So, any idea that solves a problem is definitely a perfect one, how you implement the idea is what determines how big it could grow. So, instead of waiting to have a perfect idea; start with that little one that at least solves people's problem. You can always scale the idea later in the future. Even if the idea fails to grow into big one, you can be sure to learn a lot of things from the experiences you will gather while you were running with the idea.

There is a quote I love so well, it says, *"Follow the big energy, not the big idea."* Don't let the pressure of starting off big overwhelm you. One way to free yourself from the chain of wanting to start big is to look for that idea that you feel more enthusiastic about and kick off with it. After you've kicked off with it, be patient with it and watch it grow. You may not get results immediately, that's expected, just continue to focus on your curiosity and do the things that make you feel energized.

Publicize, publicize, publicize

After you have started with that small idea, what's the next thing you need to do to make the idea big? Your next line of action should be to get the word out to as many people as possible. Publicize it, show it to people, that's the way to make your small idea big. In the past when entrepreneurs have ideas, they spread them by word of mouth. They attend hangouts and talk about their ideas, etc. but today, social media has changed the way we do a lot of things. These days, it is not difficult to get a lot of people to know about the project you are executing on social media. All you need is to be active on social media and watch how the platforms help you blow your idea.

But before getting social, there is one thing you really need to do, else your efforts on social would be wasted – you need to understand your industry inside out. If you are a thought leader in your industry, you will speak with authority anywhere you are, and once people see that you speak with authority, they trust that you have something to offer them. Nobody wants to have anything to do with amateurs, no matter what. So, learn about your industry; by so doing, you will be building a lot of credibility and you will definitely earn the trust and respect of potential customers.

After making yourself a thought leader in your industry, it is time to get social, talk about your ideas on social media, let the majority of your updates on social media be about your ideas and the things you are doing. Make noise about it on social media, no matter how awkward the idea sounds, you have to own it both online and offline.

There is something I have discovered among young entrepreneurs, they often want to hide what they are doing from others; that's not a very good thing to do. Your idea should be the life you live every day. As you have dreamed and conceived it, make noise about it both online and offline, and it won't be long before people start taking interest in what you do. And once people have started taking interest in what you do, you are already on your way to making something really big.

There are a lot of influencers on social media these days who can create massive buzz about your product, most times, for free and other times for a little fee. Reach out to these influencers, they could be bloggers, or just other media influencers, have them say something really important about your product or service and watch how your online presence explodes exponentially.

You see, you don't necessarily need to spend a lot of money before you can build a lot of buzz about your product; that was why I talked about starting with social media. What is really important is that you find where your audience is and connect with them there. These days, social media seems to be where everybody is, so start with social media. Remember that the people on social media are not the most patient people out there; they don't have a split second to wait and listen to what you are saying, so you have to make anything you are saying as interesting as possible. The best thing is to find social media users where they are and intercept their activities with your messages. By intercepting their activities with your messages, you are forcing them to listen to what you have to say. Apart from social media, there are other ways you can build buzz about your product, and I'll continue to talk about these other methods in the next paragraphs.

Apart from using social media to create a huge buzz about your activities, there are other things you can do to help advertise what you do. One of these things is giving freebies. Human beings by nature love to get things for free. You love freebies, I love freebies, and everybody loves freebies. Giving freebies doesn't mean you should give away your product or that you should render your services for free, no, there are a lot of ways you can provide free stuff to people and they will appreciate your efforts.

There is one thing about giving freebies to people – it forces the person at the receiving end to feel indebted. Human beings often want to reciprocate the kind gestures they receive from others. For instance, when you help people or give them something for free, they appreciate the help and say something like, "*I think this free stuff was good, I would need more help.*" And by needing more help, it means they will definitely come to you for more help, and when they come to you for more help, you charge them fees.

I said earlier on that you don't necessarily need to give out your product for free or render your service for free, all you need is to brainstorm something your audience might find interesting or relevant. For instance, if you run a service where you use technology to dispose of waste, you could create small pamphlets and distribute to locals where you educate them on the importance of proper waste management. It is a kind of inbound marketing of some sort because you are making the customers be the ones to talk about you and your business instead of you being the one talking about yourself.

In addition to the above methods of creating buzz about your business, you can also go the traditional way. By the traditional way, I mean, you can issue an opinion, give a speech on a current issue. No matter the means you are using to create a buzz about your business, you just need to make sure that the campaign you are running makes sense for your business and brand in terms of relevance and the message. In today's highly competitive world, authenticity is very critical. If you are perceived not to be authentic, your audience will simply dismiss your message.

Many times, young entrepreneurs are tempted to want to run paid ad campaigns for their new businesses in a bid to create a huge buzz about the business. But this is not the best way to create a buzz, moreover, you may not have all the money to continue running paid advertisement campaigns. When you are just starting your business, running paid ad campaigns may not be your best bet when it comes to creating a buzz about your business. The PR firms are going to promise you heaven on earth, but they are simply after your money and once they get it, they don't bother getting your business to be in the press as they often promise. You may run paid advertisement campaigns at a later time, but when you are just starting, word of mouth and the other means of creating publicity for your business remain your best options. When you run an advertisement campaign for a week, for instance, after the one week elapses, what becomes of your brand? You go back to square zero, but by using word of mouth, social media and the other traditional methods I have talked about above, your business will always be in people's face.

I must mention that entrepreneurship is not easy, no phase of running a business is easy, advertisement inclusive, but we still have to do it. I started an entrepreneurship Club in 8th grade in my school (Basis independent Silicon Valley) and it was really hard. One thing I noticed was that most of the people in the club were just forced into it. I don't believe anyone should be forced into entrepreneurship. If you are really an entrepreneur, you wouldn't need that extra person to push you into it. This is one of my hardest challenges in this club; most of the kids just want to come here because their parents are forcing them into it.

There are a lot of people with different ideas in the world. I was able to get 5 groups started in my Entrepreneurship Club. They were groups of people who all have different ideas completely separate from each other. I was able to start getting them into a product teaching them how to pitch to investors and hopefully start their own company. By the end of this year, they will walk out with confidence feeling that they are ready to be entrepreneurs and change the world. And these are young children. I always wanted to empower young children and I wish that I had someone who did same for me. But the sad part is most of the students don't have someone to empower them too. They are just left alone as weird and just ignored by the society. To parents, if your kid can't get good grades, that doesn't mean that your kid is a failure, that doesn't also mean that your kid won't be successful in other spheres of life. All that just means that they have to try harder in that region where they are lagging behind or they are interested in something else that's taking them away. Now, as a parent, it is your responsibility to fix that.

Anyways, let's get back to how to make something big; after you have gotten a good way to create a huge buzz about your business, you need to start pitching it to investors. For example, one of my companies was to teach little children and high schoolers about entrepreneurship. I started to go to libraries because I knew that schools wouldn't take it. To make something really big out of your idea, you have to find where the audience you want to serve is and get your business out to them. Start finding those target places of yours. And learn how to pitch to investors because that's where you are getting all your money from. And trust me on this, if you are really passionate about it, you will do great. You will make wonders.

Chapter summary

All along in this chapter, we have been looking at how to make something big. It is good that you have that idea that can shake the world; that can change the world, how do your turn it into something really big? It is the dream of every entrepreneur out there to make something big. In fact, this tendency of wanting to make something big is rooted in our human nature of always wanting more. Yes, every one of us always wants more, the billionaires always want more money, we always want to have more just like *Oliver Twist*.

As an entrepreneur, I explained that there are three things you need to do to make your idea grow into something big. First, I talked about starting small, *"follow the big energy, not the big idea."* It is like growing up and jumping up. If you grow up, you will remain up, but if you jump up, you must definitely crash land. When you take that small idea and create a business around it, you are growing with the idea, but if you just want to create something big overnight, you will crash land. So, take a small idea, breathe life into it, make it a part of your existence, channel big energy to the propagation of the small idea and watch it mature to something big.

After you have started with the small idea, I noted that you need to create a buzz about the business you have created out of the idea. We learned that there are many ways to get your business out there to people. At the beginning phase of your business, you don't want to start spending huge unavailable fund on paid advertisement campaigns. In addition to word of mouth, get social, create a huge buzz about your business on social media. The bulk of your posts should always have a way of promoting your business.

Lastly, you need to pitch to investors. These are the three ways of making something big out of your idea. First, start small, second, create a buzz about it, and lastly, pitch to investors. Notice that I didn't talk much on pitching to investors because that will take a whole chapter, so instead of scratching the surface, I have dedicated the next chapter to talk about how to pitch to investors.

Chapter Four
How to pitch to investors

"Nobody likes to hear it, because it's dull, but the reason you win or lose is darn near always the same - pitching."

— Earl Weaver

Investors are the main keys to your success. And pitching to investors is something that both and old entrepreneurs find difficult. But it shouldn't be so; if you don't know how to pitch your ideas and your business to investors, then it means you have not really gotten yourself deeply involved in the business. You need to learn how to pitch your business because it is something you are going to be doing almost every minute. Why do I say that pitching your business is something you will be doing every minute? Because besides pitching to investors, you also need to pitch to potential co-founders, you need to pitch to potential employees, you need to pitch to potential customers, you need to pitch to family and friends; in fact, you need to continue pitching to everyone. You see why you need to learn how to pitch your business, it is really important.

Pitching is basically explaining your business, and you have to do this explanation in such a way that those you are pitching to understand your business, you also have to do it so that they understand what you want from them.

Do you need them to buy into your idea so as to invest? Do you want them to be a part of your team? Basically, everything someone needs to know about your business are the things you should cover while pitching to them.

You can pitch anywhere, you can pitch to your friends and family over a cup of coffee, you can pitch to investors at events and groups. No matter where you meet the people you want to pitch your business to, one thing is common, you have to make sense within the first two minutes that you are pitching to them. In this chapter, I won't be talking about pitching to family, friends, grandmas, grandpas, etc., I would rather be talking on how to pitch to investors who will fund your ideas and startups.

Why am I dedicating much time to talk about pitching to investors? Because without the funding that comes from these investors, your idea is as good as dead. Many times, I see people conceive really nice ideas and the ideas die a natural death, why? No funding. Many people have conceived great ideas that would have changed the world but because they lacked the knowledge of how to pitch their ideas to investors, the ideas died a natural death. For that your great idea to not die, you have to fund it and to fund your idea, you need investors.

The two minutes pitch

In pitching to investors, the first two minutes of your presentation is very important, it is the time you have to really prove to your audience that you know what you are doing. It is the time you arouse the interest of your audience and have them asking for more. Investors believe that if you have an idea, that you should be able to talk about your idea in two minutes. They believe that you don't have all the time in the world to talk about your business if the idea is really worth it. So the two minutes you get to describe your business could be the most important two minutes of your life as an entrepreneur. Your performance within this two minutes is what could get people to say, *"Oh, that's interesting, I would want to hear more"* or *"I would like to hear more, contact me next week so we could sit down and talk some more about your business plan."* So within the first two minutes, your audience is going to be listening attentively like a hungry lion waiting to pounce on you if you fail to provide answers to the question of "what," "why," and "how" of your idea. Because you only have two irredeemable minutes to make a first impression when pitching your ideas to them, I want to talk about how to pitch to investors in two minutes.

The most important thing you need to do in the two minutes is to get people to like you and your idea. It is only when they like you and your idea that they can decide to have more talks with you. The two minutes is not a time to talk in details about your business plan; that should be reserved for when you have gotten their interest. So you have to take your time to make sure that your first two minutes is so powerful so that people would be willing to open their arms to receive you. One of the things you need to make your two minutes memorable is a script.

Why a script?

To do a pitch presentation without a script is like acting a movie without a movie script. You will just be going in circles without making any meaningful progress. After going in circles, you will arrive at the exact place where you started. The same way it is important that you write a script when making a movie is the same way it is even more important that you write a script when pitching your ideas to investors. If you don't have a script ready, you will keep going in circles and that's not what you want. Besides writing a script, you also need to memorize the script so you don't have to keep referring to the script at every point. Memorizing your script will help you maximize time because those few seconds you spare looking at your script also counts.

There are three parts to the script you need when pitching your ideas to investors;

- The opening,

- The middle, and

- The close

The opening is where you grab their attention and leave them asking for more like our dear *Oliver Twist*. This opening part is really important as it is where you make a first impression, and you know what they say about first impressions, *"you never get a chance to correct a wrong first impression."*

The middle part of your presentation is where you go into further details and tell them what you do, who's on your team and a little bit more information that you think they need to hear.

Then there is the last part which is where you make a closure. This third part is where you need to employ your marketing tactics and include a really strong call to action. This call to action tells them what you want from them. If you want their business card so you could book an appointment with them later to talk more about your business, the closing part of your presentation is where you do that.

I just gave a little overview of what the opening, the middle, and the closing part of your presentation should look like, let's go ahead to look at what individual components should appear in each of these parts of your presentation.

The opening part

Over the years, I have found out that people are very weak when it comes to having an attention-grabbing opening presentation when pitching their business to investors. And like I said earlier, it is the opening part of your presentation that is going to determine if people will be willing to listen to the other things you have to say.

When opening their presentations, everybody just seems to be saying the same thing. But in business, uniqueness is very important, from the uniqueness of your idea to the uniqueness of your presentation. Because everyone is opening their presentation with, *"Hello, I am Taarini, I am the CEO of Entrepreneurship*

Club...," doesn't mean you should open your presentation that way. You don't want to do what every other person is doing. If you keep doing what every other person is doing, you will get the same results they are getting. And if they are getting negative results, you will get negative results as well.

Instead of opening your presentation the same way every other person is opening theirs, add a twist to it. Set a "*hook.*" By setting a hook, I mean you should include something that will make the person or group you are pitching to say something like, "*this sounds interesting, I would like to hear more.*" Let me go ahead to talk about how you can set this hook.

The hook you are to set is specifically supposed to give your audience a hint of what the problem is that your idea is seeking to solve, or the unmet need that you are trying to meet with your idea. I am not saying that you are supposed to tell people what you do right at the beginning of your presentation, but you can still introduce what you do at the beginning of the presentation in a very special way that most people in the audience wouldn't even notice what you have done.

When you stand before investors to pitch your ideas or business to them, you have to understand one thing – these investors have listened to many of such presentations. They have read a lot of books, and they have been involved in the funding of many businesses, both the ones that failed and those that succeeded. Because of their past experiences, you need to tell them something different to stand out. You need to do something different that they will not forget in a hurry. By doing something different, I don't mean you should stand on your hands and raise your legs up. No, you should rather be bold and tell them something really unique, something memorable to give them a good reason to want to pitch their tents on your idea.

Now, the only way to be different from everybody else is to do things that not everybody is doing. I want to go ahead and explain how you can do things differently from everybody else.

Use stories

Have you ever thought about the impact that a little short story is going to make in your presentation? It can make a whole lot of difference. But this is not something that most entrepreneurs do. What most entrepreneurs do is to get on a platform, introduce their selves and start yapping away about what their business is about. But there are a lot of things you can do with stories – with stories, you add a personal feel and touch to what you are saying. Stories help convince the people you are talking to that you have truly been involved in your business. It doesn't need to be a long story (in fact, you don't even have the time for that), just something short and relevant is all you need. And if you present the story at the beginning of your presentation, there is no way you won't get the investor hooked and also have them want to hear more. After all, we all love to hear the end of every story. You could tell a story of why you are in business, you could also tell a story of how you came about the name of your company; you could also tell a story of how you came about your logo, your tagline, or just any story that's relevant to your business. The bottom line is to tell a story at the beginning of your presentation. It is a good way to differentiate you from the others. The other people don't tell stories, they just start talking about their business as if they are reading a news on TV.

Use analogies

Besides telling catching stories, you can also use analogies to describe what your business is all about and there is nothing that hooks investors the more than these two – stories and analogies. Imagine that you have a startup where you help businesses receive their payments using cryptocurrencies, and someone walks up to you and asks what you do? I am going to give two possible answers and leave you to choose the one that strikes the loudest chord.

Reply 1: *we help business fasten their financial transactions same way social media is helping them in their advertising.*

Reply 2: *we help businesses develop solutions that help them receive payments in cryptocurrencies.*

Now, everybody knows what social media is, and how it is changing the way traditional advertisement is done, everybody also understands what it means to fasten financial transactions, but does everybody understand cryptocurrencies? The answer is no. the first reply used an analogy to compare your business with what everybody is used to. And it is a better way to hook an investor to want to hear more since you have given them a clearer understanding of the things you do.

Use similes and metaphors

In addition to stories and analogies, you need to also have similes in your opening script. Remember the whole idea of having all of these in your script is to hook your investor and have them want to hear more about your idea. Also, make use of metaphors.

Metaphors can be so strong that you can use them throughout your whole presentation and summarize with the metaphor being the last thing that they hear. If you are going to make a lasting impression with your pitch presentation, all the elements above must be included in the opening part of your presentation.

Analogies, similes, and metaphors help you to use everyday terms or words to explain in plain terms what your business is about without having to go into the deep technicalities of your business. The analogies, similes, and metaphors you have in your presentations could be all you need to send a message to your audience that you truly know what you are saying and it is a good way to help you stand out from the others. You don't want to make it appear like you are reading points from a slide.

Now, that's it about the opening part of your pitch presentation. In a nutshell, I said you should hook your audience with the opening part of your presentation, and to do that, you need to incorporate stories, analogies, and metaphors. Note that the best analogies, similes, and metaphors are the ones that have nothing to do with the business you are doing. If you are creating a social networking platform for people with special needs, don't say something like, *"we are going to be the Facebook for people with special needs!"* If you say that, it means you are already making some technical comparison between your product and some other existing product which isn't what you want. Even though your idea may be totally different from that of Facebook, including Facebook in your analogies may make your investors assume that you are copying an already existing concept. Remember, investors are looking for unique ideas to fund. And that's it for the opening part of your pitch presentation.

The middle part of your two minutes pitch

If you have done well and set a good pace with the opening part of your presentation, you may not have a lot of problems taking care of the middle part of your presentation. There are a number of models that you could use to develop the middle part of your pitch presentation. The model I am going to show you employ the use of questions to get the investor to want to hear more about your business.

Here are six important questions you need to answer in those two minutes:

Remember that the whole idea is to get the investor say something like, *"this sounds interesting, I want to hear,"* and you can only get investors to say it if you answer the six questions correctly.

Question #1: *What is your product or service?*

This is the number one question after you have done your opening. You have told your stories, you have used analogies to buttress your points, it is time to tell the investors what your product or service is.

Question #2: *Who is your market?*

It is very important that people know who your market is. When they know your market, they can be able to determine if the market is huge enough to make you and them money. Remember that investors don't run charities, they are also looking to recoup their investment; so they want to be sure that your business has the required market to help them recoup their investment.

Question #3: *How will you make money?*

The answer to this particular question goes hand in hand with your answer to question two above. Now that the investors know who your market is, they also want to know how you want to make money from this market using your product or service. As I said earlier, investors are not people who run a charity, they are investing in your idea because they want to get a return on their investment, and if you don't tell them how you are going to make money, there is no way they are going to invest in your idea.

Instead of getting into the deep technical aspects of your business, cut the long technical stories, investors don't want to hear them, they want to hear how you are going to make money so that they too can make a return on their investment. This your way of making money has to include a thorough analysis of laid down plans that you have mapped on how to make money with your ideas.

Question #4: *who is behind the company?*

Here, you are to give a brief description of the people who are going to build your company with you.

Question #5: *who are your competitors?*

You don't have to necessarily call them out by name or by category; the important thing is that you recognize that you have competitors out there. In addition to admitting that you have some competitors out there, also mention that the problem you are solving with your idea is one that your competitors have never thought about.

For instance, you could say something like this, *"yes, we have some formidable competitors out there, but I want to assure you that what we are doing is something that none of them have ever thought about."* The whole idea is to recognize that you have competitors and hammer on what you do that these competitors are not doing.

Question #6: *what's your competitive advantage?*

This particular question is a very big one because here, you have to name one or two things that you are doing that other people out there are not doing. Remember that you just admitted that you have competitors in your answer to the last question, the point now is, *"what's that particular thing that you are doing which these competitors are not doing."* If your competitors are selling orange and you are manufacturing orange juice, you have to say why your orange juice should be preferred when people could simply get orange and lick away. Sometimes, this is the most difficult question you have to answer and you must not give a shallow answer.

Now, you are done with the opening part of your presentation, you are also done with the middle part, what you have left is the closing part.

The closing part

The same way you don't just start your pitch presentation with some cliché phrases is the same way you shouldn't just end it by saying, *"Okay, thank you..."* That's not good enough and is really a cheap way of ending your presentation.

To close your pitch presentation in a powerful way, you have to do the following:

1. Ask

The Christian Bibles says and I quote, "*Ask, and ye shall find, knock and the door shall be opened unto you.*" Did you notice that the first word is "*ask?*" If you are like most entrepreneurs who just assume that their audience knows what to do, then you must have wasted the time you spent talking about the opening and middle part of your script. Don't be like most people who don't ask; don't assume that your audience knows what to do. Remember, "*Ask and ye shall find.*"

If you want their business cards to talk with them later, ask; if what you want is to have an appointment with them next week, ask. Do you want to know if they have any interest in the things you have just said, then ask. Do you want a reference? Do you want to sit down and talk about your business in more details and get an expert opinion? Ask! Again, "*ask and ye shall find.*"

There are people who have problems when it comes to asking for what they want, if you are among these people, there is a way out. You can get someone who is good at sales to help you come up with a good way to ask what you want. The bottom line is that no matter how you do it, you need to ask for something. Don't just close your pitch presentation without asking for something.

2. Leave them with a thought you would want them to remember

Lastly, before closing, you have to leave your audience with a thought that you would want them to remember, and once you have done that, you thank them and exit the stage.

For example, if I have just finished pitching Entrepreneurship Club to some investors and I want to leave them with something to remember, I could say something like, *"In conclusion, we would like to leave you with one thought: as you go home today and meet those awesome kids, do know that today, you heard about a club that can nurture them into great Entrepreneurs who can change the world with their ideas. Thank you very much."*

With the above lines, I have put something in the mind of my investor such that anytime they see kids, they recognize that they have heard something about nurturing kids into becoming Entrepreneurs and they would want to act.

In summary, in making your two minutes pitch presentation stand out, you need to memorize your scripts and rehearse the things you have there over and over again until they become part of you. Furthermore, as you are presenting those points to an investor or bank of investors, you have to make your enthusiasm and passion for your idea come across. It is very important that you make your passion and your enthusiasm for your business or service come across. The reason is that if you don't communicate your passion and transfer your enthusiasm to your audience; you are just like everybody else, and that's definitely not what you want. You have to think about how you are presenting and not just what you are presenting.

Chapter summary

In this chapter, we have been looking at how to pitch your ideas and business to investors. I said that the two minutes pitch is the best if you want to grab the attention of your audience. You don't need 60 hours to explain what your business is all about unless you are not enthusiastic about the business. If you are enthusiastic and passionate about your business, you should be able to know how to communicate your passion and transfer your enthusiasm to your audience in two minutes.

Remember that you have to stand out from the crowd with your presentation. And I explained that you can do that through incorporating stories, using similes, analogies, and metaphors especially at the beginning part of your presentation. In making use of stories, similes, analogies, and metaphors, you have to look at your audience and their cultural differences so that you don't make use of stories, similes, and metaphors that convey a different meaning from what your audience is used to.

The six questions you have to answer in the middle part of your presentation are very important. Prepare answers to the questions beforehand and rehearse them over and over again. The sixth question is particularly very important and you should pay a lot of attention when crafting an answer to the question.

Furthermore, you have to close by asking for what you want. Don't just assume that your investors already know what you want. Even if they may already know, they still want to hear it from you. Remember that the only people that find are those who ask. So, ask and ye shall find.

Rehearse, rehearse, and rehearse. If you are going to come across to your investors as someone who is passionate and enthusiastic about their idea; if you are going to come across as someone who is credible, you have to rehearse. Rehearse those questions and have them at your fingertips. Continue to rehearse until you are able to communicate your passion and transfer your enthusiasm to your investors. You can dedicate two hours or an hour every day to rehearse your presentation. You can do this two weeks or a week before your actual pitch presentation. While rehearsing it, use your phone to record yourself and play the recording later to pinpoint places where you are not getting it right. Continue to rehearse until you have gotten everything right.

Finally, no matter how good you think you are as a presenter, you need to get a coach to help you organize your thoughts. Every industry out there has coaches – life coaches, presentation coaches, etc. Find a coach, have somebody look at what you are doing and offer expert suggestions.

You have simply learned how to pitch your ideas to investors. What you have learned in this chapter can be used to pitch to family members, friends, angel investors, or just about anybody who you want to pitch to. No matter the person you are pitching to, you just need a good opening, a good answer to a couple of questions in the middle and a good closure.

In the next chapter, am going to talk about something really important that affects entrepreneurs, both young and old.

Chapter Five
Be humble

"There is nothing noble in being superior to your fellow man; true nobility is being superior to your former self."

— ***Ernest Hemingway***

Now that you have learned these four major topics, the next major ingredient you need to make something big as an entrepreneur is to be humble. Humility is a quality that I see lacking in many entrepreneurs. Many times I see entrepreneurs especially the young ones that after achieving some level of success start raising their shoulders, start feeling on top of the world, and start feeling like they are above every other person. If you fall in this group, you have to know that no one got anywhere by being overconfident and being mean.

You should always be ready to learn from others, you should always be ready to get the most knowledge you can from anything. Whether it be a history or whether it be a conversation or anything, being an entrepreneur is not just making the product and selling it, it is about how you are different from others. What makes you great, what makes you nice and open to the public, what's so great about interacting with you? The reason why you are so great is that you have a secret power. Your secret power is to be humble, to be nice, not to be overconfident, and to be down to earth.

Have you ever noticed how down-to-earth *Mark Zuckerberg* is? He owns a big company yet every few weeks, he does a Q&A session with normal people who sometimes do not even work at Facebook. Most times, he does this because he wants to learn more about other people's thoughts and ideas. And not just him, there are a lot of people who think like that, there are a lot of people who work like that and they reap the immense benefits derived from being humble.

I can't stress this enough, even when you feel you have arrived, you need to still add one more ingredient to your recipe, and this ingredient is humility. As an entrepreneur, you are a leader automatically, and there is nothing that makes an effective leader more than humility. Whether it is a team or individual setting, humble people always make the most effective leaders and often tend to be high performers, because there are a lot of things that humility helps a person achieve that being overconfident cannot.

Some people often confuse humility and low self-esteem, but they are two entirely different things. Many people think that being humble means thinking less of themselves. However, being humble doesn't have anything to do with thinking less of oneself, rather, it has more to do with thinking less about oneself. Have you seen the difference now? If you have low self-esteem, you are thinking less of yourself, but if you are humble, you think less about yourself and think more about the people around you. When you are humble, you are kinder, more self-aware, more charitable, and more compassionate.

Furthermore, humble leaders don't tell lies about their limitations and strengths. They truly recognize their strengths and acknowledge their weaknesses and often seek ways of improving on those areas where they are lacking. They are supportive without being submissive, they are open-minded without being obstinate, they are confident without being conceited. With the all these listed qualities of a humility, it is clear to see that what makes a great leader is not necessarily the personality of the leader but their ability to show humility.

In what ways are you supposed to show humility as an entrepreneur? There are many ways you can show humility as an entrepreneur. The good thing is that all these are going to increase your effectiveness and productivity as an entrepreneur and a leader.

Humility listens

Earlier, I said that *Mark Zuckerberg*, the owner of the largest social networking platform organizes an occasional Q&A with common people – those who are not involved with his company. To what end? To listen to people in a bid to get new ideas. That's not all, he occasionally throttles round the world meeting young developers at code camps, where he engages them in discussions and they share ideas. Why do you think he does all of these? He understands the importance of listening, he recognizes that it is better to listen than to speak.

For any relationship to thrive, be it a romantic relationship, family relationship, or the relationship between an entrepreneur and their clients, an entrepreneur and their employees, listening to the opinions and the ideas of others must be an integral part of the relationship. When you listen to others as an entrepreneur, be they your customers, or your employees, it is an indication that you respect their opinions, and that you are receptive of their ideas.

As an entrepreneur how do you listen? By actively seeking feedback from your local community, colleagues, and most importantly, your customers. When you are doing that, you are indirectly getting ideas on how to improve your product and service, you are also boosting employee morale.

You don't necessarily need to be in a face-to-face conversation to actively listen to what the other party is saying. We are in a digital age, and there are now a lot of avenues through which you can listen to the opinions of those around you about your brand and service. Remember that active listening is sure to dramatically improve your humility quotient.

For instance, when you are on social media, do you care to read all the things that people are saying about your brand? Apart from engaging in face-face-conversations, social media is a nice place to hear of all the things that people are saying about your products and brand in general. Do you make out time to read all the comments that your followers are leaving? There are no better ways of listening to the opinions and ideas of others than that.

A rule of thumb here is to listen more than you speak. As an entrepreneur, you are definitely going to gain more by listening than you would gain by talking all the time. When you are talking, you are simply speaking what you already know, but when you actively listen, you are likely to add more ideas and knowledge to your current knowledge base. Listen more, it doesn't necessarily portray you as someone with low esteem but as someone that is humble and someone who respects the opinions of others.

Humility tests

Humility doesn't just assume that it is right. As a humble entrepreneur and leader, you should always be willing to test your assumptions even though they are in line with your instincts. Instead of blindly sticking to one strategy and believing that it works, test out different strategies to know the one that works most.

For instance, if you have been sending one pattern of email with the same pattern of crucial elements like subject and body, and you have not been recording a lot of success from the email marketing efforts, do you just continue doing the same thing or test out other strategies? A humble leader and entrepreneur is not rigid, rather he tests out different strategies and finds out the one that works best. Being unnecessarily rigid even when your methods are not working is a quality of arrogant people and narcissists.

As an entrepreneur, you should be humble enough to always test every opinion and new ideas and always stick to that which works best. When you listen to people and have learned some new ideas and suggestions from them, don't discard these new ideas and opinions, rather, put them through a test to sieve out those that could be useful to you.

Humility admits

No one of us is infallible, we all have our faults, weaknesses, and error, but admitting these errors, weaknesses, and errors is where humility comes in. When you give out an instruction that later leads to a bad outcome, do you admit that it was your fault and assume responsibility, or do you shift the blame to someone else? Many times, entrepreneurs feel that admitting their errors is a sign of weakness, but that's not true, it is actually an act of gumption, generosity, and grace.

When you are humble enough to admit that you did something wrong, you are creating room for yourself to improve and make better decisions. Furthermore, when you admit that you don't know everything, you are indirectly indicating that you need help. When you indicate that you need help, you are showing your willingness to learn, and there is nothing better than always adding to your knowledge base. When you have a large knowledge base, you make better decisions and also empower others around you to be better people.

Besides increasing your knowledge, admitting your weakness also helps you gain the trust of others. When you admit an error today, you work together with your team to correct the error so it doesn't metamorphose into something bigger tomorrow. So, the next time you stumble, own it; your honesty and humility will surely pay off.

Chapter summary

In this chapter, we have seen that humility is an important trait that you must possess if you truly want to be successful as an entrepreneur. Being unnecessarily pompous will take you nowhere, being unnecessarily overconfident will take you nowhere too. Look at the most powerful entrepreneurs today and learn humility from them. Bill Gates is an embodiment of humility, same can be said of Mark Zuckerberg. I don't want to start naming all the popular entrepreneurs together with their different acts of humility, I want to leave you with that responsibility.

No matter how far you have gotten your brand, no matter how big your idea grows, without the ingredient of humility, then something is seriously missing in your success recipe. As an entrepreneur, you should always be quick to listen, test out new ideas that you have learned, and you must always admit your weaknesses and seek out means of correcting them. These are qualities of a humble person

Even though that being humble is not something that is very easy, especially in a world where humility can be misunderstood to mean low self-esteem, you have to remember that it is absolutely essential. When you add humility to your toolkit, the result you get is an all-round success.

In the next chapter, we are going to learn something really important – how to measure entrepreneurship in units.

Chapter Six

Measuring entrepreneurship in units

"It is an immutable law in business that words are words, explanations are explanations, promises are promises — but only performance is reality."

—***Harold S. Green***

I am glad you have gotten this far in the book. To reward your efforts, I want to throw in one more topic – how to measure entrepreneurship in units.

Picture yourself at a gas station to fill up your car's tank, and there is no way to measure the amount of gas you have dispensed. What do you think would happen? Either you get less gas than you had intended or you get more than you had intended. This goes to show that measurement is very important.

In life, we must always measure our performance against different metrics; this measurement allows us to know when we are going in the right direction and when we are supposed to retrace our steps.

In sciences, for instance, measurement is very important. It is never taken for granted, that's why units of measurement is one of the first topics that science students are usually taught in school.

As a science student in 8th grade, I have been learning about units of scientific terms, example, Force is measured in Newton, Energy in Joules, and Distance in meters, etc. That made me wonder: is there a unit that is used to measure Entrepreneurship? I started to do online research to see if I could find something meaningful, but nothing of such was available on the internet. I also asked Silicon Valley Venture Capitalists and CEOs of successful startups, but they had no answer either.

I started to question: *Entrepreneurship is among the most pervasive activities of human beings, so why is there no way to measure it?*

I believed strongly that there should be a way to measure entrepreneurship so that when the entrepreneur measures venture against different metrics, he/she can know where they are getting it right and where they are supposed to retrace their steps.

Then, I even asked myself: *why do we actually have to measure Entrepreneurship?* And the answer was clear after a few days of digging in. The answer is same as why we need to measure or size up anything else, whether it is money, resources, distance, force, etc. If we don't measure these, we won't know where we are and what goals to set. We can't compare any company or country to another one.

Furthermore, if there is no way of measuring entrepreneurship, an entrepreneur wouldn't have a restraining factor when they are doing certain things. And once there is no restraining factor, entrepreneurs could choose to handle their business in many careless manners, and that, in turn, could affect their employees, and their community.

So, to help entrepreneurs have a way of measuring their performance, I was able to develop a framework for measuring entrepreneurship.

By the way, this chapter (and probably some other chapters in this book too) are not just applicable to students below 18 years because it could be beyond their scope. My hope is that this method of measuring entrepreneurship will become the standard for how we rate startups and any other venture in the world.

Since I humbly feel that I am inventing something new here, I am calling the unit of entrepreneurship as my name – **Taarini**. So, Entrepreneurship will be measured as **Taarinis**.

Now, let's talk about how to measure it. It goes into the "***WHYs***" of entrepreneurship. The key reasons why a person starts an entrepreneurial venture are 3-fold: ***be your own boss***, ***create wealth*** and ***make an impact in the world***.

So, along these lines, I have created the following as the 4 factors of Entrepreneurship:

- **Wealth creation (W)**: this encompasses revenue creation, cash generation, and profit making.
- **Impacting the world (I)**: Jobs created (J)
- **Customers touched (C)**: a company that doesn't impact customers is not doing its job; that is why I feel this is a critical factor in this calculation.
- **Ethics (T)**: success without ethics is incomplete.

I am giving a maximum score of 10 on a scale of 1 – 10 to each of the 4 variables above. The minimum score is 1, you can have a score of 1 or 2 or 3 but cannot have a score of 2.3. The reason is that I want companies to feel motivated to deliver to the next performance level to get the next score.

So, Entrepreneurship **(E)** formula is:

E = W x I x C x T

The maximum value of E is 10 X 10 X 10 X 10 = 10,000 Taarinis

The minimum value of E is 1 X 1 X 1 X 1 = 1 Taarini

Of course, if you are not an entrepreneur, you have a score of E as 0.

Why did I decide to multiply the 4 factors, instead of some other formula? I feel that some companies can create millions of dollars of wealth but remain small in employee size or customer count and hence have no impact on the world other than themselves. They may get acquired for, say, a billion dollars due to smart technology but they never created jobs or touched too many customers.

Now, let's define how to quantify each factor:

Wealth Creation (W)

Every company starts out with a score of 1. If the revenue of the company (not of the individuals) is equal to or greater than $100 Million, then they get a full score of 10. The company will remain at a score of 1 till you reach $10M on this metric in any year. This is a threshold to go up the scale of W beyond 1. Between 1 and 10, you can pro-rate the score, depending upon the dollar number. If the company is at $50M, they get a score of 5.

I am capping it because I feel $100M is a large enough number to prove that you have a viable business model and have delivered a product that can get paid nicely. Please note that I have intentionally not put paper valuations as this metric. Because, I see a lot of Silicon Valley startups that have < $10M in revenue but command valuations of $100M or even more. But I don't think that is the right metric for entrepreneurial success. Companies need to generate revenue at scale to be meaningful. For example, companies like Google, Alibaba and Facebook will easily get a score of 10 today on W metric.

I also thought into if I should have a separate unit for countries outside the US and I decided not to. I feel that the number of $100M is pretty universal for showing a strong and repeatable business model.

Impact (I)

I strongly believe that creating wealth for yourself is useless and is an opportunity wasted. So, I included the factor of jobs created in this metric. If you don't make an impact by creating jobs, then there is no point in being an entrepreneur. If you create equal to or greater than 10,000 jobs, I give you a score of 10. If you create 1000 or lower jobs, you are at a score of 1. So, 1000 jobs is the threshold to rise above a score of 1 – I feel it's fair because otherwise, you have not made enough of an impact to deserve a higher than 1 score. Similar to W, you slide up the scale proportionately beyond 1 as you increase the job count from 1,000 to 10,000.

Customers Touched (C)

I feel that too many startups or other ventures miss out on this because of the cushion of venture capital. The real form of funding for any company is customer revenue. If you touch at least 1,000 paying customers, you have achieved a good scale and hence get a full score of 10. You start at a score of 1 and remain there till you have 10 paying customers. A paying customer is defined as a customer who is paying for your product or services with at least an annual contract signed. So, pilot customers do not count here. Similar to W and I, you slide up the scale proportionately beyond 1 as you increase the customer count from 10 to 1,000.

Ethics (T)

This is the most critical metric, in my humble opinion. I strongly believe that any company that achieves revenue and growth without ethics has done a meaningless job because it is then breeding a company culture that is poisoning the society. For example, a company like *Uber* will get a score of 1 due to all the recent allegations around treatment of women. Similarly, *Google* will get a score of 1 due to firing its employee *James Damore* for openly expressing his views on the poor diversity culture. Such actions of the co-founders and CEOs of a company have a negative impact on employees and the larger community.

In fact, I was even toying with the idea of giving a score of 0.5 for this factor because a poor ethics company with extremely high revenue should have a negative impact on its

E score. But I decided to keep the threshold at 1 to be consistent with other factors. The Ethics score will be measured by two factors: 1) gender pay equality and 2) any allegation of discrimination against any employee of the company or the company as a whole. For Ethics scoring, I would like to follow the Intel Capital definition of Diversity which includes women, underrepresented minorities, LGBTQ community, people with disabilities and military veterans. I chose this definition because it is more inclusive than other definitions of diversity. A company can get five points on Ethics score if they publicly show equal pay being given to their diversity employees on the same pay grade as other employees. I would like a company to show this metric every year to keep getting that score. If they don't show in a particular year, they lose these points immediately.

If there is no allegation of discrimination against any employee or the company as a whole in a particular year, the company gets four points. Once there is an allegation, the company loses those points. But if it proves in a court of law that the allegation was incorrect, then it gets the points back.

Hence, the scale on Ethics score can be a minimum of 1 and maximum of 10.

Use the framework to rate yourself

It is necessary that every entrepreneur uses the framework as explained above to rate their performance against all the metrics.

Note that you can't do this yourself, as you won't be honest to rate yourself accordingly. Get an external body and have them rate your venture.

When having an external person rate your venture, you are only to supply them with your revenue. Allow them to figure out the other metrics by themselves. This way, the external evaluator gives an honest rating.

The external person has to interview your staff to be able to have a basis for rating you against the Ethics metric. They also have to independently determine how you have been impacting your immediate community. The bottom line is that you should only provide them with your revenue and allow them to determine the other metrics by themselves and give you an appropriate rating.

I must reiterate that you can't rate your business by yourself, you must have an external body rate you and give feedback.

Now, after the rating, what next? After obtaining your rating, your next action should be to evaluate your performance and make improvements if you have not scored above average. Even if your performance is above average, you still need to improve and put more effort into making sure that you don't drop in ratings.

If it is in the area of wealth creation that you have scored low, go back to the drawing and think up more ways of turning your ideas into cash. The truth is that this particular metric is the hardest to fix, the others can easily be fixed if there is a will.

If it is in the area of ethics that you have scored low, endeavor to identify the different areas that your business has not been doing well ethically in. Identify the root and solve the problem from the bottom up.

Look out for all the areas where you scored low and fix them all. Your aim should be to run a business that creates wealth in the most ethical manner and impacts lives. If you do that, you have a thriving business on all counts.

Chapter summary

Like scientific terms, I believe entrepreneurship should have a unit of measurement. And I have tried in this chapter to develop a framework that can be used to measure entrepreneurship. The framework identified four factors of entrepreneurship to include wealth creation, impacting the world, customers touched, and ethics. Have an external body rate your business against these four metrics and make amendments accordingly.

Conclusion – I did it, you too can

"A conclusion is simply the place where you got tired of thinking."

– Dan Chaon

Despite the many challenges that young entrepreneurs face in the society, I was able to scale through and have been leading some businesses successfully. In the book, I highlighted many of the problems I faced and how I was able to overcome many of them. If I did it, you too can.

It is true that the society does not want us to be entrepreneurs. The society wants to bully us into conformity, it wants us to keep following a certain pattern. We can break the many barriers that the society had set before us. No law says that one must be in their 40s before starting a business, no law says that those under twenty can't start businesses. In fact, there are many notable young entrepreneurs under twenty who started and are still running their successful businesses up till today. I can go on and list some of these notable entrepreneurs.

Away from myself now, let me talk about other young entrepreneurs who are doing exploits not minding the many barriers that the society has placed before them. At just six years of age, *Cory Nieves* became the owner of *Mr. Cory's Cookies*. He first started by selling hot cocoa in his home country, Englewood. He would later go on to selling cookies and lemonade because he wanted to save money for college. Mr. Cory's cookies have no preservatives and come in a variety of colors and he sells them through his website. Cory was inspired to be an entrepreneur because he was tired of taking a bus to school and wanted to make enough money to buy a car.

What of *Robert Nay*? Didn't he launch his "*Bubble Ball*" a mobile game app in 2010 that received more than a million downloads in 2010 when he was just 14? Now, who says you can't make something big as a kid? Nay's game is a physics-based game, and even though he had no coding experience before creating the game, he still beat the odds that were against him and through research at the public library, he learned everything he needed to know to write the more 4,000 lines code base of his mobile game. All these he did in one month. His game now helps students learn spelling and sight words.

I can't continue to list other young entrepreneurs who have done something really meaningful. Their information is on the internet and a simple Google search will lead you to all the inspiration you need. One thing is common among all of them – they were able to move above the barriers set against them by the society. After they have moved past the barriers, they were able to make something really big.

You too can change the world, you are not too young to do it. Don't let what the society is saying hold you back. Many people are going to see you as weird, that doesn't change anything. You are going to suffer social rejection. It is not easy, but if you are able to build a good support system around yourself, you will always overcome every obstacle.

I believe the book has provided you with every information you need to go out there and change the world. Grab the information, put everything in practice and watch the sky be your starting point.

Made in the USA
San Bernardino, CA
22 February 2019